smile

GABRIELA HERNÁNDEZ-FRANCH

BOOK SERIES BY FIG FACTOR MEDIA

WordPower Book Series

© Copyright 2021, Fig Factor Media, LLC.
All rights reserved.

All rights reserved. No portion of this book may be reproduced by mechanical, photographic or electronic process, nor may it be stored in a retrieval system, transmitted in any form or otherwise be copied for public use or private use without written permission of the copyright owner.

It is sold with the understanding that the publisher and the individual authors are not engaged in the rendering of psychological, legal, accounting or other professional advice. The content and views in each chapter are the sole expression and opinion of its author and not necessarily the views of Fig Factor Media, LLC.

For more information, contact:

Fig Factor Media, LLC | www.figfactormedia.com

Cover Design & Layout by Juan Pablo Ruiz
Printed in the United States of America

ISBN: 978-1-957058-01-6
Library of Congress Control Number: 2021923563

DEDICATION

I dedicate this book to my beautiful family: you all are my biggest reasons to smile. Los amo!

ACKNOWLEDGMENTS

I'd like to greatly thank Jackie Camacho-Ruiz for always listening to her divine downlands and sharing this special opportunity with us. You rock! Thank you to the entire Fig Factor Media team for helping us bring our books to life and for all the work, love, and planning that went into creating this new series. Thank you to Kylie, Marie, Anna, and JP for your selfless work!

A big shoutout to my husband, Donald, for being so supportive in everything I do. You are my rock and cheerleader in all things. I love you. Thank you to all my friends and family who inspire me and remind me of the simple and beautiful things in this life; the ones that really matter. I thought of you all as I wrote this book.

INTRO

A smile can be such a simple concept. An ordinary, simple gesture part of regular life. Something that too commonly we take for granted. After all, what power do thirty-two pearly whites really have? Despite this, I believe a smile has the power to change people's lives.

- One smile can begin a beautiful friendship that can last a lifetime.
- One smile can remind someone that life is worth living when they're at their lowest.
- One smile can captivate attention so deeply that someone falls in love at first sight.
- One smile can brighten someone's confidence so much they change their life's mission.
- One smile can be the reason someone chooses to follow their dreams and live authentically.

In my life, I've experienced moments where a smile has made all the difference. I hope to share some with you today so that by the time you close this book you too can identify moments when a smile has truly made an impact in your life. I invite you to keep on smiling. You never know—it just may even change your life!

WHAT IS A SMILE?

Verb: To form one's features into a pleased, kind, or amused expression, typically with the corners of the mouth turned up and the front teeth exposed.

Noun: A pleased, kind, or amused facial expression, typically with the corners of the mouth turned up and the front teeth exposed.

A noun that can turn into a verb that can be changed into an adjective. The possibilities to use your smile are truly endless.

It's an action. It's a gesture. It's a gift. It's a smile.

A SMILE'S INCEPTION

Have you ever wondered why babies are born without teeth? One could say because they simply don't need them in the first months of their lives.

Yet, have you ever wondered why babies are born knowing how to smile? It's true, babies naturally are born with this ability. At first, it's unconscious, an expression they know just as they know how to cry. But how beautiful that before we can walk, talk, or are fully developed, we know how to smile and use it to communicate. Our smiles have been with each one of us since the beginning. Our smiles are truly our first language!

A JOYOUS OCCASION

Smiling is contagious. Smiling is irresistible. When you see someone smile it's natural for you to want to smile back. It's such an organic reaction. Can you imagine celebrating a special moment and not smiling? It's impossible! How silly would we look if we didn't grin when we received good news? Our smiles are always present in moments of joy. Joy and smiling go hand in hand. It's important to recognize that these moments of joy are what make life so precious.

Our smiles are unique, have extraordinary power, and are with us in the best moments of our lives.

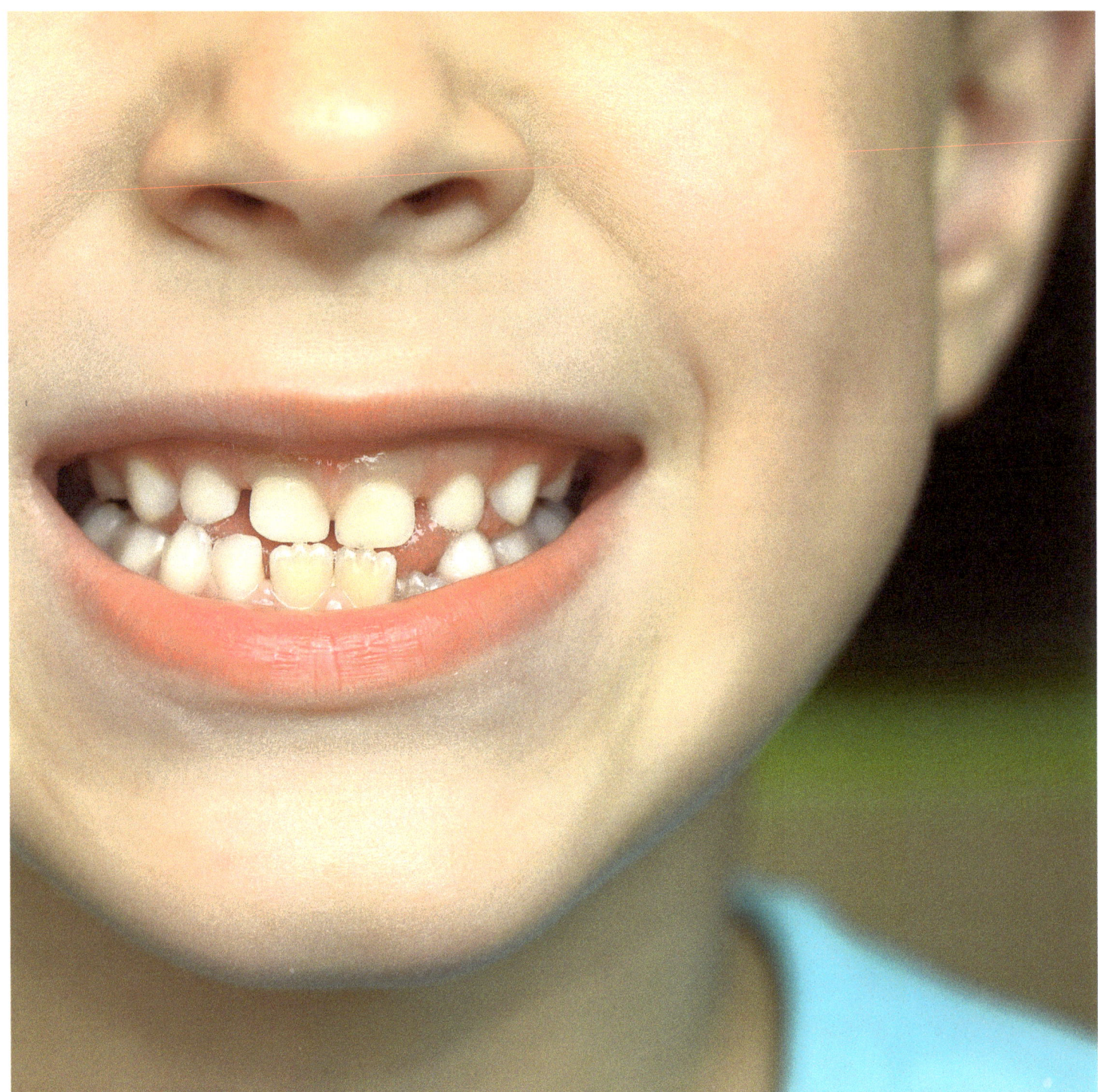

THE IMPERFECT SMILE

When I was younger, I loved candy a bit too much, and my baby teeth began to get cavities. Due to this, a few of my baby teeth began to decay. Since I was growing and needed them, pulling them out was not an option. The solution? Remove the cavities and fit my teeth with silver crowns. Once I got all my crowns in, I remember thinking, "*I have a very unique smile. No other kid I know has silver teeth!*"

While I do remember accepting my reality, of course kids would point out my shiny imperfect teeth. Who wouldn't? I had grills in kindergarten! Thankfully, during that time we all began to lose our baby teeth and we all had funny and incomplete smiles anyway.

Once my adult teeth came in, I made sure to appreciate and show off my smile even more. I finally had teeth that all matched! This is one of the reasons why I love sharing my smile with others!

A SMILE A DAY, KEEPS THE DOCTOR AWAY!

Not only does smiling make you more attractive and approachable, but smiling has many other benefits as well!

- Smiling decreases blood pressure and releases endorphins[1]
- The boost in endorphin output forces us to breathe deeper, resulting in a calmer outlook and increased coping ability
- Smiling can help boost the immune system by decreasing stress levels
- Smiling can make us live longer and happier lives
- Different types of smiles let you communicate lots of things
- Smiling is contagious and can have an instant impact to those around you

Simply put, smile more!

---

[1] "National Smile Week: 10 Fun Facts about Smiling," Community Home Health Care, August 10, 2015, https://commhealthcare.com/national-smile-week-10-fun-facts-about-smiling/.

WHO'S SMILING NOW?

Life always has funny ways of showing you important lessons.

It was a normal Saturday night in my college dorm lounge, and a few close friends were with me chilling and celebrating early for my 20th birthday. Board games, music, food, the dorm works. It was then time to sing me "Happy Birthday" and eat cake. I smiled, happy to be surrounded by good friends. I blew out the candles, made a wish, and then it was time to bite the cake. This is a Mexican tradition where you bite a small piece of cake first and at times those around you can jokingly push you into the cake to try and give you a face full of frosting.

Next thing I heard.... BOOM!

As I went to bite, my friend tried to push me into the cake but my seat accidentally slipped back and made the cake move forward. Instead, my friend had slammed my face right onto the hard table. Ouch.

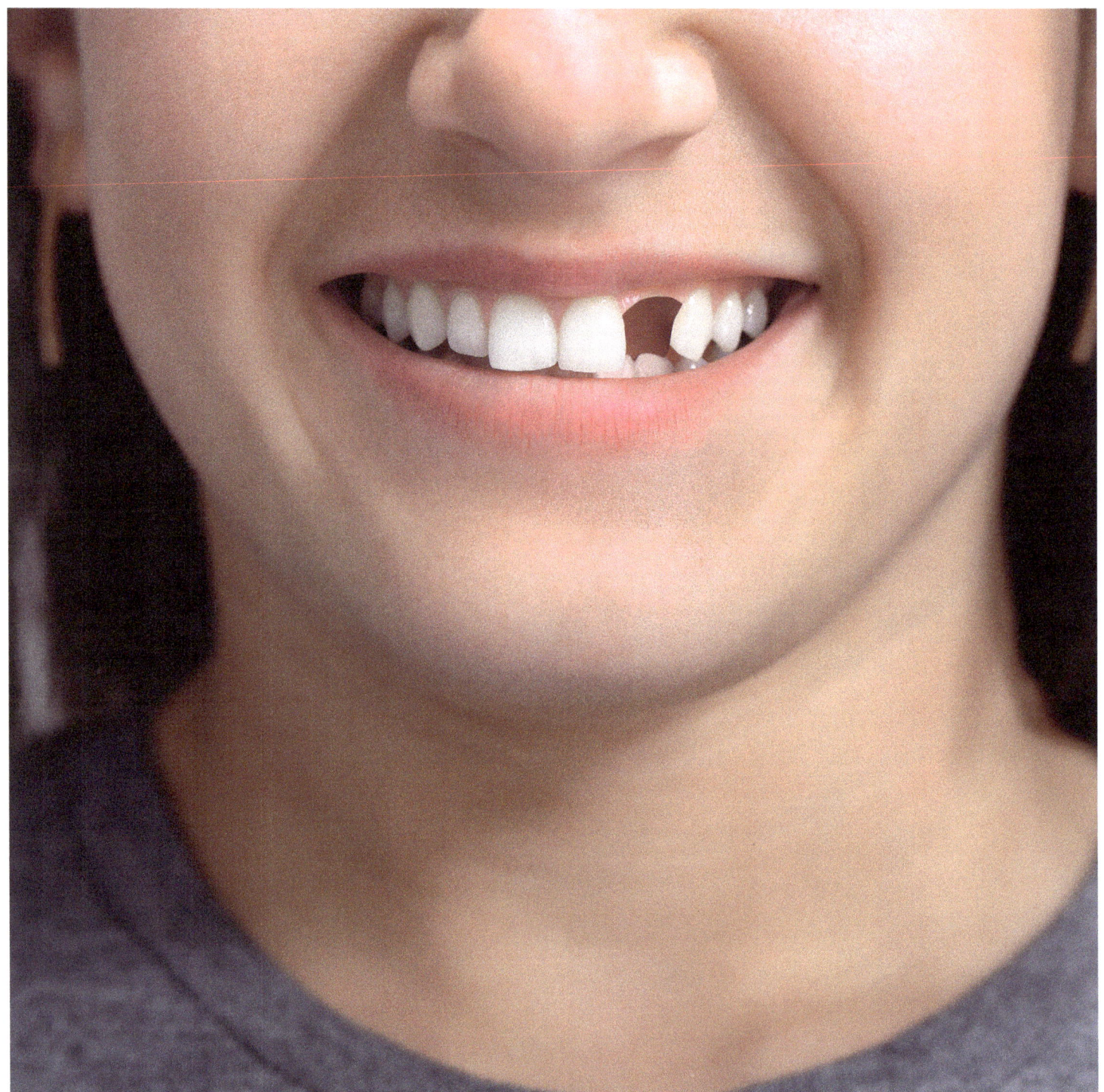

A BROKEN SPIRIT

Everyone gasped and I was convinced I heard my nose break. I rushed to the sink with my hands on my face. No blood anywhere—a good sign I thought. I didn't even feel pain because I was in shock. But then, my tongue felt something that wasn't right. I jerked my hand to my mouth to feel a gap between my teeth. Tears rolled down my face and I wouldn't move my hand out of my mouth. My smile was broken. My heart was broken.

What came after was pure torture. I couldn't see my dentist until days later. What was once my favorite thing to do now became forbidden fruit. My confidence dropped to the ground. I felt as if my identity had evaporated and was lost. I couldn't face anyone. I was beyond embarrassed and had to wear a scarf and cover myself the entire time. Those were some of the longest days of my life.

NEW CROWN. NEW SMILE.

This experience was truly eye-opening for me. It was a fresh reminder of how important my smile really is and how much it means to me. As a friendly, outgoing person, I realized how much I use my smile and how it is truly a part of who I am. The moment that was taken from me, I couldn't be me. This made me understand how impactful our smiles truly can be for our confidence, self-esteem, and for our self-love.

After a long journey that involved my tooth becoming infected, getting a root canal, having multiple temporary crowns, and getting my final porcelain crown, I had my smile back.

I'm extremely thankful for the work and impact dental professionals have on our lives. I am grateful for their desire to help others have the best and healthiest smiles they can have. They rock!

P.S. This is your reminder to schedule a dental checkup! You'll thank me later.

MY SECRET WEAPON

My smile is my superpower,
My tool of construction.
Even in silence my smile is loud,
It makes a big entrance bright and proud.

When my mind can't think fast enough,
My smile is ready to do the talking.
Words can get stuck in translation,
But grins are their own representation.

Ever hear a sweet baby laugh?
Don't tell me you didn't smile.
Laughter is a beautiful thing to hear,
Joy, happiness, bliss appear.

The impact is endless, the stories are many,
My secret weapon is sharpened and ready.
Remember my smile, it's one of a kind.
I may be biased but it's the best one you'll find.

FIND YOUR REASON TO SMILE!

I can assure you; you have many reasons to smile. Yes, it's no secret that many things in this world can bring us down. There's suffering, pain, injustice, crime, sadness, fear, and so much more. It wouldn't be life if we didn't experience these moments.

Yet, in times of anguish there's always something that can bring us comfort and put a smile on our face. What memory from your childhood makes you smile? Was there a moment you shared with your family or friends that always brightens your day? What's your favorite ice cream flavor or food that makes you lick your lips just thinking about it? Sit and make a SMILE list. Grab your journal or a notebook and write all the reasons you have for smiling. When you are feeling down, look at your list to remind you that it too shall pass. Life has given you beautiful reasons to smile.

THE POWER OF A SMILE

"A smile enriches those who receive it, without impoverishing those who give it."
– Dale Carnegie

"Everyone smiles in the same language."
– George Carlin

"Nothing you wear is more important than your smile."
– Connie Stevens

"Use your smile to change the world. Don't let the world change your smile."
– Unknown

"Smile, it is the key that fits the lock of everybody's heart."
– Anthony J D'Angel

DON'T BE SHY! SHARE THOSE PEARLY WHITES!

My hope for you, dear reader, is that this book reminds you of how beautiful and important your smile is. Sure, it might have imperfections but don't let that stop you from using the best gift you have. Use your smile to create new friendships, to fuel your relationships, to share your inner beauty and essence. I've been told often that I'm photogenic and I like to think that the reason for this is because I always smile for pictures. Share those pearly whites! I invite you to take that selfie with a big smile, post it online and share your smile with the world! We all can use more smiles today! Use the #SmileWordPower as you post. I look forward to seeing those beaming, vibrant smiles!

And, as Mother Teresa said:
"Let us always meet each other with a smile, for the smile is the beginning of love."

ABOUT THE AUTHOR

Gaby Hernández Franch is a first-generation college graduate and in her short career she has worked in various fields including education, financial services, and most recently marketing and publishing. Gaby joined Fig Factor Media, an international publishing house, and its sister company JJR Marketing in Dec 2019 and hasn't looked back since. She loves the opportunity to help others share their amazing stories and support clients with their brands and projects. Most recently, Gaby was honored with a 30 Under 30 Award from the Publicity Club of Chicago in 2020 and 2021 for her professional accomplishments.

Gaby enjoys talking the stage as an MC for events and hosting the Author Central Podcast— FFM's very own podcast. She is a contributing author for the book series: *Today's Inspired Young Latina* and *Hispanic Star Rising Vol. II*. Gaby is passionate about traveling, learning about cultures and languages, has a deep love for music and the arts, and has been part of various musical ensembles playing violin and signing.

www.ingramcontent.com/pod-product-compliance
Lightning Source LLC
Chambersburg PA
CBHW041235240426
43673CB00011B/347

© 2020 East York Press

Kõik õigused kaitstud. Ühtegi osa raamatust ei ole lubatud kopeerida ega kasutada ilma autoriõiguste omaniku kirjaliku loata, välja arvatud tekstilõigud, mis on lisatud arvustusele.

Kaanepilt Angela Melgaard.
Eesti keelde tõlkinud Ene Timmusk.

Tänan, Tontu!

BROMLEY SWITZER | VIRVE ALJAS-SWITZER
PILDID ROBERT ASKEW

EAST YORK PRESS

Meie armsatele karvastele sõpradele,
nii endistele kui praegustele -
me ei unusta teid iial.

Unised laupäeva hommikud, kui on raske voodist üles saada.

Kes tuleb ja poeb mulle kaissu?

Tänan, Tontu!

Külmetavad varbad hommikukarguses!

Kes toob
mulle sussid?

Tänan, Tontu!

Varahommikused jalutuskäigud parki.

Kes annab mulle hoogu juurde?

Tänan, Tontu!

Meile meeldib hommikusöök,
aga mitte koristamine.

Kes aitab nõud puhtaks pesta?

Tänan, Tontu!

Hunnikute viisi pesemist ootavat musta pesu.

Kes aitab seda sorteerida?

Tänan, Tontu!

Nädalalõpud, mis on täis asjaajamisi.

Kes proovib mind panna sellest rõõmu tundma?

Tänan, Tontu!

Mullivann aitab meid peale toredat päeva puhtaks saada!

Kes hoiab silma peal, et kõik pestud saaksid?

Tänan, Tontu!

Õhtusöögid pere ringis toovad meid üksteisele lähemale.

Kes vaatab, et meil ei jääks toitu üle?

Tänan, Tontu!

Lõõgastume üheskoos lemmiksaateid vaadates.

Kes lõõgastub eriti palju?

Tänan, Tontu!

Karvased kallistused enne kiiret nädalat.

Kes toob mulle ilusaid unenägusid?

Tänan, Tontu!

Kes on tegelikult Tontu
Tontu on üks väga armas koer, kelle nimi on Frank
ja kes elab Torontos oma emme Bromley'ga.

Talle meeldib kõige rohkem visatud asju tagasi tuua, ujuda ja olla
perega - just selles järjekorras.

East York Pressi teisi teoseid

See raamat on mõeldud kõigile, kes igatsevad oma lähedaste järele.

Kui mäletada neid, kes on kaugel, ei lahku nad tegelikult kunagi meie juurest.

Priya ja Jay jagavad oma lugusid kasutades nende akende vahele tõmmatud konservikarpidest ja nööridest valmistatud telefone. Priya on väga õnnetu, kui saab teada, et Jay ning ta pere kolivad ära väga kaugele.

Kasutades ära oma leidlikkust, mõnda üles harutatud kampsunit ja tuhandeid sõlmi, avastab Priya, et ükski vahemaa ei saa sõpru teineteisest eemal hoida.

See raamat on saadaval teistes keeltes.
Vaata EastYorkPress.com

EAST YORK PRESS

www.ingramcontent.com/pod-product-compliance
Lightning Source LLC
Chambersburg PA
CBHW041235240426
43673CB00011B/348